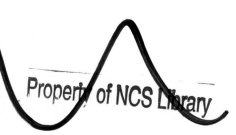

# SOME MAJOR EVENTS IN WORLD WAR II

## THE EUROPEAN THEATER

**1939** SEPTEMBER—Germany invades Poland; Great Britain, France, Australia, & New Zealand declare war on Germany; Battle of the Atlantic begins. NOVEMBER—Russia invades Finland.

**1940** APRIL—Germany invades Denmark & Norway. MAY—Germany invades Belgium, Luxembourg, & The Netherlands; British forces retreat to Dunkirk and escape to England. JUNE—Italy declares war on Britain & France; France surrenders to Germany. JULY—Battle of Britain begins. SEPTEMBER—Italy invades Egypt; Germany, Italy, & Japan form the Axis countries. OCTOBER—Italy invades Greece. NOVEMBER—Battle of Britain over. DECEMBER—Britain attacks Italy in North Africa.

**1941** JANUARY—Allies take Tobruk. FEBRUARY—Rommel arrives at Tripoli. APRIL—Germany invades Greece & Yugoslavia. JUNE—Allies are in Syria; Germany invades Russia. JULY—Russia joins Allies. AUGUST—Germans capture Kiev. OCTOBER—Germany reaches Moscow. DECEMBER—Germans retreat from Moscow; Japan attacks Pearl Harbor; United States enters war against Axis nations.

**1942** MAY—first British bomber attack on Cologne. JUNE—Germans take Tobruk. SEPTEMBER—Battle of Stalingrad begins. OCTOBER—Battle of El Alamein begins. NOVEMBER—Allies recapture Tobruk; Russians counterattack at Stalingrad.

**1943** JANUARY—Allies take Tripoli. FEBRUARY—German troops at Stalingrad surrender. APRIL—revolt of Warsaw Ghetto Jews begins. MAY—German and Italian resistance in North Africa is over; their troops surrender in Tunisia; Warsaw Ghetto revolt is put down by Germany. JULY—allies invade Sicily; Mussolini put in prison. SEPTEMBER—Allies land in Italy; Italians surrender; Germans occupy Rome; Mussolini rescued by Germany. OCTOBER—Allies capture Naples; Italy declares war on Germany. NOVEMBER—Russians recapture Kiev.

**1944** JANUARY—Allies land at Anzio. JUNE—Rome falls to Allies; Allies land in Normandy (D-Day). JULY—assassination attempt on Hitler fails. AUGUST—Allies land in southern France. SEPTEMBER—Brussels freed. OCTOBER—Athens liberated. DECEMBER—Battle of the Bulge.

**1945** JANUARY—Russians free Warsaw. FEBRUARY—Dresden bombed. APRIL—Americans take Belsen and Buchenwald concentration camps; Russians free Vienna; Russians take over Berlin; Mussolini killed; Hitler commits suicide. MAY—Germany surrenders; Goering captured.

## THE PACIFIC THEATER

**1940** SEPTEMBER—Japan joins Axis nations Germany & Italy.

**1941** APRIL—Russia & Japan sign neutrality pact. DECEMBER—Japanese launch attacks against Pearl Harbor, Hong Kong, the Philippines, & Malaya; United States and Allied nations declare war on Japan; China declares war on Japan, Germany, & Italy; Japan takes over Guam, Wake Island, & Hong Kong; Japan attacks Burma.

**1942** JANUARY—Japan takes over Manila; Japan invades Dutch East Indies. FEBRUARY—Japan takes over Singapore; Battle of the Java Sea. APRIL—Japanese overrun Bataan. MAY—Japan takes Mandalay; Allied forces in Philippines surrender to Japan; Japan takes Corregidor; Battle of the Coral Sea. JUNE—Battle of Midway; Japan occupies Aleutian Islands. AUGUST—United States invades Guadalcanal in the Solomon Islands.

**1943** FEBRUARY—Guadalcanal taken by U.S. Marines. MARCH—Japanese begin to retreat in China. APRIL—Yamamoto shot down by U.S. Air Force. MAY—U.S. troops take Aleutian Islands back from Japan. JUNE—Allied troops land in New Guinea. NOVEMBER—U.S. Marines invade Bougainville & Tarawa.

**1944** FEBRUARY—Truk liberated. JUNE—Saipan attacked by United States. JULY—battle for Guam begins. OCTOBER—U.S. troops invade Philippines; Battle of Leyte Gulf won by Allies.

**1945** JANUARY—Luzon taken; Burma Road won back. MARCH—Iwo Jima freed. APRIL—Okinawa attacked by U.S. troops; President Franklin Roosevelt dies; Harry S. Truman becomes president. JUNE—United States takes Okinawa. AUGUST—atomic bomb dropped on Hiroshima; Russia declares war on Japan; atomic bomb dropped on Nagasaki. SEPTEMBER—Japan surrenders.

# WORLD AT WAR

# Battle of the Coral Sea

# WORLD AT WAR

# Battle of the Coral Sea

By G.C. Skipper

 CHILDRENS PRESS, CHICAGO

The U.S.S. *Arizona* burns after the surprise Japanese attack on Pearl
Harbor in December of 1941.

FRONTISPIECE:
Photographs show the Japanese aircraft carrier
*Shokaku* under attack and burning on the last
day of the Battle of the Coral Sea.

Library of Congress Cataloging in Publication Data

Skipper, G. C.
  Battle of the Coral Sea.

  (His World at war)
  1. Coral Sea, Battle of the, 1942—Juvenile
literature. I. Title. II. Series.
D774.C63S55      940.54'26      80-25088
ISBN 0-516-04787-6

It was almost five months after Pearl Harbor. The Japanese had taken giant strides in the Pacific. Guam, Wake Island, and Hong Kong had fallen to them in late December, 1941. Manila, Singapore, and Bataan were theirs by mid-April, 1942.

Now the Japanese were ready to begin Operation MO. This plan had two parts. First the Japanese wanted to take Tulagi, a small island in the Solomon Islands chain near Guadalcanal. Then, they would attack Port Moresby on the southeast coast of New Guinea. From Port Moresby it would be easy to launch an attack against Australia.

The Japanese Fourth Fleet was divided into several parts for the invasion. First there was a Tulagi invasion group. This included transports, destroyers, minesweepers, and other ships. They would leave from Rabaul, New Britain and steam to Tulagi.

RUSSIA

*SEA OF JAPAN*

KOREA

JAPAN

*YELLOW SEA*

CHINA

*EAST CHINA SEA*

Okinawa

Formosa

*LUZON STRAIT*

LUZON

INDO-CHINA

*SOUTH CHINA SEA*

Philippine Islands

BORNEO

CELEBES

*JAVA SEA*

*BANDA SEA*

*TIMOR SEA*

*ARAFURA SEA*

NEW GUINEA

AUSTRALIA

Aleutian Islands

PACIFIC THEATER OF WAR

M

1,300 miles to H

*PACIFIC OCEAN*

Bonnis Islands

Iwo Jima

Wake

Marianas

Eniwetok

Marshall Islands

Caroline Islands

Gilbert Islands

New Britain

Solomon Islands

Ellice Islands

New Hebrides

*CORAL SEA*

Fiji

New Caledonia

Noumea

Norfolk

NEW ZEALAND

Another similar group would head toward Port Moresby the following day. A third group of ships would escort both invasion forces. This third group included light cruisers, heavy cruisers, destroyers, and a light aircraft carrier, the *Shoho*. Also steaming toward the Coral Sea were two huge aircraft carriers, the *Shokaku* and *Zuikaku*. These two Japanese carriers were the most powerful of all the Japanese ships in the area.

The harbor of Rabaul, New Britain, was the launching place for the Japanese force that invaded the island of Tulagi.

The two American officers who planned the defeat of the Japanese in the
Coral Sea were Admiral Chester Nimitz, commander-in-chief of the United
States Pacific Fleet (left), and Admiral Frank Jack Fletcher, who
directed the fight aboard the aircraft carrier *Yorktown* (right).

American Intelligence had broken the Japanese
code. Through messages the enemy sent, the
Americans knew a big move was planned.

"Looks like something's happening in the Coral
Sea," said one of the American code breakers.
"Better notify Admiral Nimitz."

Admiral Chester Nimitz was commander-in-
chief of the United States Pacific Fleet. When he
learned that Japanese invasion forces were
gathering, he contacted Rear Admiral Frank Jack
Fletcher. He ordered Fletcher to make sure the
Japanese plans for the Coral Sea would fail.

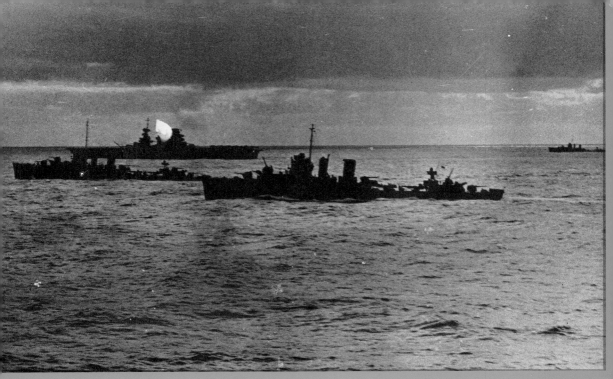

The ships that made up Task Force 17 assembled in the southeastern part of the Coral Sea.

Fletcher was at sea aboard the aircraft carrier *Yorktown*. Destroyers and heavy cruisers served as the *Yorktown's* escort. Joining Fletcher's forces were another American aircraft carrier, the *Lexington*, and her escort vessels. This group of ships was called Task Force 17. On May 1, 1942, Task Force 17 gathered in the southeastern Coral Sea.

The Americans and their allies, the Australians, guessed that Tulagi was one of the Japanese attack points. On May 1, the few Australian troops there left Tulagi. They would have had no chance against a large invasion force.

This picture, taken from the *Yorktown,* is of the United States oiler *Neosho,*
as she refuels the carrier. The *Neosho,* a slow craft, was nicknamed
"Fat Lady." She was sunk by the Japanese a few days after this picture was taken.

For the next two days Task Force 17 took on fuel from oil tankers and prepared for battle. On May 3 Fletcher received an urgent message. The Japanese had taken Tulagi! Fletcher took the *Yorktown* and the ships that had refueled and moved northward toward Tulagi. All night they moved across the waters. The next morning they were close to Tulagi. It was 7:00 A.M.

"Get the planes out of here," Fletcher commanded. "We've got work to do."

Planes from Task Force 17 on their way to Tulagi.

Immediately the planes began warming up. They took off from the decks in waves. In no time they had reached the small island. There, they attacked. Bombs screamed. Machine guns chattered like angry magpies.

The Japanese there were surprised. They were building a seaplane base on the island. Work halted as they fought back.

This American plane pulls away after attacking Tulagi. The island can be seen below.

A captured Japanese naval map once helped Japanese officers plan their attacks and defenses. The map shows American bases and ships.

The American attack destroyed or damaged a few Japanese ships. But most of the invader ships had left Tulagi. However, the raid did bring the American fleet to the attention of Vice Admiral Takeo Takagi. Takagi now knew for sure that a large American force was in the area.

Takagi ordered his strike force southward to meet the Americans. The carriers *Shokaku* and *Zuikaku* and other ships in the Japanese striking force moved out. Takagi meant to destroy the American fleet.

15

The sailors and fliers of both fleets waited tensely for the enemy ships to be located.

The two mighty fleets neared each other. There was great tension aboard all the ships. Hundreds of miles of ocean separated them. But at any time an enemy search plane might locate them and send in an attack.

For the next two days the fleets failed to find each other. The ships ducked in and out of rainstorms. The clouds made the job of the search planes more difficult.

Then, on the morning of May 7, some of the clouds cleared. A Japanese pilot was searching the water. When he looked down he saw American ships.

"The enemy!" cried the pilot. He was very excited. "Quick, make the report. We've found the enemy!"

The excited Japanese pilot reported that he had spotted American aircraft carriers and cruisers. But he was wrong. He had sighted an American oil tanker, the *Neosho*, and *Sims*, an American destroyer.

But his news was enough for Takagi. He was sure the enemy had been found. Takagi ordered waves of high-flying bombers and dive-bombers to attack.

Japanese planes zoomed down toward the ships. They rained down bombs. They swished torpedoes across the water. Soon the destroyer had sunk and the oiler was adrift. The Japanese pulled back.

An American plane, almost hidden by the smoke from the Japanese carrier
*Shoho*, banks in to attack.

However, Takagi was about to meet trouble.
While he was attacking minor targets, the
Americans had found real prizes. The carrier
*Shoho* and her escort had been located!

The Americans launched masses of airplanes
from the *Lexington* and *Yorktown*. They were ready
for a hard-hitting bomb and torpedo attack.

"There they are!" cried an American pilot. "Just
like sitting ducks!"

A torpedo finds its mark—the side of the *Shoho*. Many bomb and torpedo hits resulted in the *Shoho*'s sinking.

Below them was the Japanese light carrier *Shoho*. With their planes' engines at a fever pitch, the Americans swarmed down on the Japanese. They let go a deadly hail of bombs and torpedoes. The *Shoho* was hit by a half-dozen torpedoes and a dozen bombs. Suddenly she exploded. She jerked, swerved, and then gurgled as she sank.

"We've done it!" cried the American pilot. He radioed back to the ships, "Scratch one flattop!"

The airplanes are back on the deck of the *Lexington* after their successful strike.

The Japanese were stunned by the terrific American attack. They moved all their ships away from the battle area.

Then the weather turned bad again. Rainstorms danced everywhere. No one could see anything. For a time the two fleets drifted in blindness.

"Can you find them?" asked Takagi.

"No, sir. We've lost contact," replied one of his officers.

"Get Rear Admiral Hara a message," Takagi demanded. "Ask him if he can launch a night air attack."

"Yes, sir!" replied the Japanese officer. He ran to the radio room.

In a short while Rear Admiral Tadaichi Hara radioed back. He had planes ready for the attack.

"Excellent!" said Takagi. "Tell him to find and destroy the enemy."

Soon the Japanese pilots were running across the decks. They climbed into their planes. The engines warming up sounded harsh and loud. One by one the Japanese planes lifted off. They disappeared into the darkening sky.

The squadron roamed the sky. They peered through the darkness. They flew and flew. The pilots became edgy.

Japanese carrier-based airplanes warming up before a mission

This Japanese squadron searches for its target.

"Can you see anything?" one of them asked.

"No. It's impossible to find the Americans now. Let's return to the ship."

"I agree," said the first pilot.

The squadron also agreed. They turned their planes around. Then they headed back to their base on the carrier.

"I hope there's hot tea waiting," said one of the Japanese.

"This night fighting isn't too bad!" joked another. He felt secure. They hadn't found the Americans. Soon they would be back on their ships, and safe. That is, until the next mission.

As the Japanese chatted on their radios, American fighter planes suddenly came out of the darkness. The talking was interrupted by the blast of machine guns. A Japanese pilot screamed as American bullets stitched his cockpit.

Japanese airplanes burst into flames. They hurtled toward the sea. Streams of black smoke licked out behind them like kite tails.

A Japanese plane hit by gunfire burns as it plunges toward the sea.

"Let's get out of here!" a Japanese pilot shouted.

The remaining planes buzzed away in all directions. In the scramble to get away, a few more Japanese planes were shot down.

The Japanese survivors quickly formed a squad as they fled into the night. The American planes were left behind them. The Japanese flew through the dark, looking desperately for their fleet.

Finally a pilot cried, "There are our ships!" Below them the fliers could see the whitecapped wake of a carrier.

The Japanese pilots were relieved. They began to circle the ship in a landing formation. The first pilot made his approach. Suddenly, gunfire erupted. The Japanese plane plunged into the sea.

By mistake, the Japanese pilots were trying to land on the American carrier *Yorktown*!

The other Japanese pilots, who were also ready to land, saw what had happened. They pulled back into the sky and disappeared.

On the night of May 7, a Japanese plane much like the one shown here was shot down as it tried to land on the *Yorktown*.

American sailors slept when and where they could
during a battle.

"Imbeciles!" Takagi raged when he heard what
had happened. "Don't they know enough not to
land on an enemy ship!" He was furious at the
foul-up. "There's nothing to do now but pull
back."

Following Takagi's orders, the Japanese moved

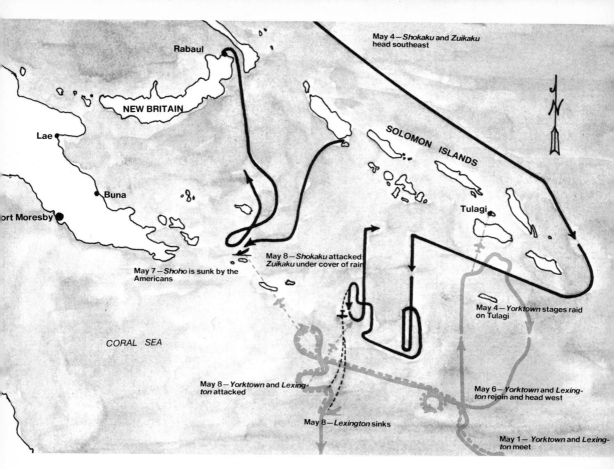

This map traces the paths of American (blue) and Japanese (black) ships during the Battle of the Coral Sea. Dates and the approximate positions of the aircraft carrier groups are noted. The paths of the *Shoho* and the Port Moresby invasion force are also shown. These two groups were turned back on May 7th.

out. They steamed north. Some hours later Takagi had them double back. When they changed directions, the Japanese were headed for the American fleet. The next day, May 8, was to be historic. For the very first time, aircraft carriers were lining up to do battle.

Success or defeat in the Coral Sea depended on the airplanes of both fleets. While the Japanese pilots were experienced, the American pilots had radar to help direct their attacks.

A "Dauntless" bomber is checked over before a mission.

Airplanes would decide this battle. The aircraft carriers of both fleets would never sight each other. There would be more than 150 miles of ocean between them!

The Japanese and the Americans each had about the same number of airplanes. They were evenly matched. The American planes had radar. But their pilots had little fighting experience. The Japanese had no radar, but their pilots had seen much fighting.

The fleets moved toward each other. American and Japanese scout planes searched the sea for signs of the enemy. Finally, at 8:15 A.M. on May 8, 1942, one of Fletcher's search planes sighted the Japanese striking force.

The American pilot circled high above the enemy ships. He counted what he saw in the water below.

Then he sent a message: "Two carriers, four heavy cruisers, many destroyers. Steering 120 degrees, 20 knots, their position roughly northeast."

"Let's go get them," Fletcher said after receiving the message. "This time we're in business."

He ordered most of the planes from the *Yorktown* and *Lexington* to the attack. They flew for a while and then came upon the Japanese aircraft carrier *Shokaku*. The *Zuikaku*, the other Japanese carrier, was about eight miles away. It was hidden by a rainstorm.

Above: The Japanese carrier *Shokaku* makes an **S** turn to avoid attacking planes. Below: Columns of water near the *Shokaku* show where bombs were dropped.

The *Shokaku* burns as the American planes continue their atacks.

American airplanes (arrows) try to finish off the *Shokaku*.

The American planes attacked the *Shokaku*. A deadly storm of bullets, bombs, and torpedoes fell. The mighty carrier zig-zagged out of the way, dodging this savage downpour.

Then dive-bombers screamed down on the *Shokaku*. Two direct hits slammed into her. Fires sprang up everywhere.

With almost no pause, a second wave of American planes joined in the fight. They, too, attacked. The *Shokaku* was hit a third time. Although many fires blazed, the Japanese sailors were able to get them under control. The *Shokaku* turned and escaped the American assault.

While the Japanese sailors were busy fighting off the American aircraft, the Japanese fliers had a streak of luck, too. They had spotted the American carriers at the same time the Americans had seen theirs.

Waves of Japanese aircraft rose from the decks of their carriers. The planes zeroed in on Fletcher's task force. They singled out the *Yorktown* and the *Lexington*, swooshing down with a rattling of gunfire. The planes' bomb-bay doors opened wide. They unloaded their bombs and swooped away.

Left: Defenders aboard the *Yorktown* wait at their stations for the Japanese attack. Below: A Japanese torpedo plane (center of picture) avoids antiaircraft fire during its attack on Task Force 17.

A bomb explodes as it hits this flight deck.

One Japanese bomb went right through the flight deck of the *Yorktown*. Fires raged across her deck. Sailors ran, yelled, and hauled out fire-fighting equipment. They finally got the fire under control.

Then the *Lexington* was hit. Two torpedoes sliced through her port (left) side. Small bombs landed on her deck. Another bomb landed on her smokestack, blowing it sky-high.

The two enemy forces fought until noon. Then, as if it had never begun, the Battle of the Coral Sea was over. A strange silence floated across the water. The noise and the screams and the ships and the planes were gone.

The Americans looked themselves over. They had lost a quarter of their aircraft in the battle. The *Yorktown* had a hole in her deck, but was not seriously damaged.

But the *Lexington* was not so lucky. After the Japanese planes had attacked, she seemed to be all right. The American planes were coming back from their mission. Some of them were landing on the *Lexington*.

But after an hour had passed, the "Lady Lex," as she was known, was shaken by an explosion. Some gas tanks had been weakened by the torpedo hits. A spark had set off the fumes.

The beginning of the end for the *Lexington*. Above: Planes were back aboard the *Lexington* after their mission, and everything seemed to be under control a few hours after the battle. Below: An airplane is flung off her deck as the "Lady Lex" explodes.

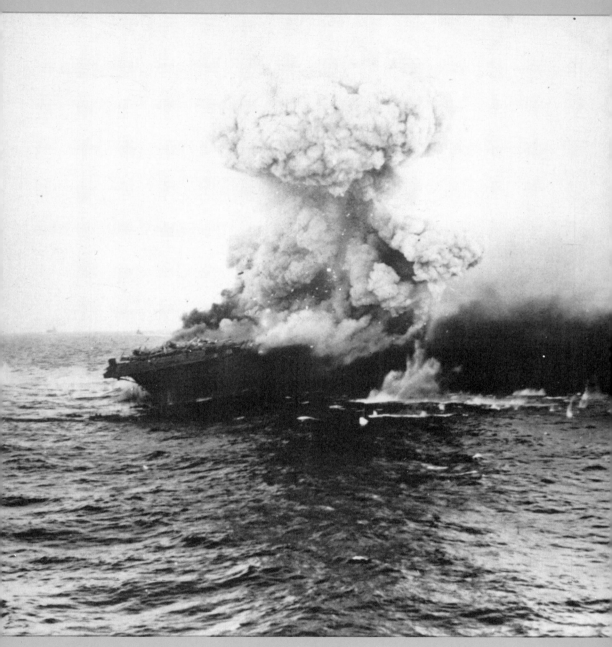

The *Lexington* burns out of control after the explosion.

Many crew members were killed by this blast. Fires started up again. The men aboard fought the flames for hours. Finally they realized that she could not be saved. The captain gave an order to abandon the ship.

The crew did not want to leave. But they followed the captain's command. They put their rooms in order. They closed offices. Then they lined up their shoes neatly before leaving the ship. They acted as if they would be coming back.

The crew dove from the decks of the *Lexington* when the captain gave the order to abandon ship.

The *Lexington*'s crew is taken aboard other American ships.

The captain was the last to leave the ship. He and the rest of the crew were taken aboard the other ships. The Americans did not want the enemy to take the Lady Lex. So, they watched sadly as an American destroyer shot torpedoes at her. She burned brightly for a time, then sank beneath the water. Some of the *Lexington's* crew cried when she finally went down. They felt that they had lost a home. Some were even "plank owners." They had served on the *Lexington* from the first day she had sailed.

Even though the *Lexington*, the *Neosho*, and the *Sims* had been sunk, the Americans felt they had done well in the Battle of the Coral Sea. Because of it, the Japanese failed in their plans. They did not take control of Port Moresby. It was the first time since Pearl Harbor that a Japanese invasion had been stopped.

Also, this battle was the first time that ships had fought without ever seeing each other. Both sides learned lessons from this carrier duel. In the future, more airplanes would be left to protect the carriers when the other airplanes were attacking the enemy. And the Americans would use their radar better. They did not intend to repeat any mistakes.

Finally, the Battle of the Coral Sea left the Japanese with only four carriers ready for war. The *Shokaku* was badly damaged. She could not be used for a while. The *Zuikaku* had lost over a third of her aircraft. She did not have enough left to carry out an attack.

Midway Island, where the lessons learned from the Battle of the Coral Sea helped the Americans defeat the Japanese

This Japanese weakness would be important in an upcoming naval battle. In another month the Japanese would try to invade Midway Island. At Midway the Americans would pounce on Japanese ships and win a great victory. And within three years the true winners would emerge.

Japan was destined to go down in defeat.

The last hours of the *Lexington*

# INDEX

*Page numbers in boldface type indicate illustrations*

*About the Author*

A native of Alabama, G.C. Skipper has traveled throughout the world, including Jamaica, Haiti, India, Argentina, the Bahamas, and Mexico. He has written several other children's books as well as an adult novel. Mr. Skipper has also published numerous articles in national magazines. He is now working on his second adult novel. Mr. Skipper and his family live in North Wales, Pennsylvania, a suburb of Philadelphia.